Angels and Dirt

Angels and Dirt

An Enquiry into Theology and Prayer

JOHN DRURY

Chaplain and Fellow of Exeter College, Oxford

Darton, Longman & Todd
London

First published in Great Britain 1972 by
Darton, Longman & Todd Limited
85 Gloucester Road, London SW7 4SU
© 1972 John Drury
Set in Intertype Baskerville and
printed in Great Britain by
The Anchor Press Ltd and bound by
William Brendon & Son Ltd, both of Tiptree, Essex

ISBN 0 232 51185 3

FOR CLARE

Contents

Acknowledgments

The author records his thanks to the publishers of the following copyright works, from which he has made quotations: To Mr Gavin Muir and The Hogarth Press for *Autobiography* by Edwin Muir and to Faber and Faber Ltd for *In Memory of Sigmund Freud* from *Collected Shorter Poems 1927-1957* by W. H. Auden.

Foreword

The most obvious characteristic of this book is that it is alive. For certainly what it gives to its readers is life—not information but life.

The life is the result of a marriage—most deeply, one may suspect, John Drury's own marriage to Clare, to whom he has dedicated the book. Not that he exhibits anything so intimate and private to the public gaze. But its result can be seen in another marriage where Drury acts as priest and officiant—the marriage of profound personal experience to theological thinking. Drury is a trained theologian. But for him theologising is not working out a set of speculative puzzles. It is a way of exploring life and of finding it by becoming aware of it. His book reminds one of Mersch's description of Augustine: 'For him thinking was not a matter of putting concepts together but of finding the truth within himself'.

It is noticeable that the language Drury uses is never abstract and general but always concrete and particular. His images and turns of phrase haunt the mind because they have all the punch of simplicity. He is always commendably precise (there is no lazy thinking here), but it is the precision of a poet who has found exactly the right word to evoke the reality he wishes to communicate. It means that he has successfully appropriated and internalised his experience and has thus been able, in the true sense, to objectify it. What therefore he gives us is wisdom —insight into the ways of God with men and of men with God. It is the kind of wisdom we need today when one of the (perhaps inevitable) results of the proliferation of universities is the attempted disguise of intellectual mediocrity by the mumbo-jumbo of intellectual pretentiousness.

Drury has made the scholar the servant of the artist. That has been true of all creative theologians. I believe, therefore, that this book is a sign that theology is finding new life and discovering that it can speak with power to all who have the courage to think—and to feel.

H. A. WILLIAMS.

Mirfield.

Author's Preface

The line of enquiry which is pursued in this book began with an open lecture under the auspices of the Theology Faculty at Cambridge in 1969. It was published by Mowbrays in 'The Phenomenon of Christian Belief' edited by G. W. H. Lampe. Readers of that book will catch echoes of it in the first two chapters of this one. I am indebted to the Faculty for getting me started. Since then I have taken things further in response to invitations to give Holy Week Lectures at the theological colleges at Wells and Cuddesdon and open lectures for the chaplaincy of the University of Kent at Canterbury. Without them I would not have gone on. Robin Baird-Smith of Darton, Longman and Todd gave me encouraging criticism in the latter stages. I owe much to the interest and kindness of the community at Pilsdon in Dorset. Last and most I thank Clare. The full effect of the sharp sympathy, the security and the freedom which she has given me is a secret which I am only beginning to understand, and appreciate with wonder.

J.H.D.
Exeter College, Oxford
Easter, 1972

CHAPTER ONE

The School of Seeing

'Sirs, if you never tried this art, nor lived the life
of heavenly contemplation, I never wonder that
you walk so uncomfortably, that you are all com-
plaining and live in sorrows, and know not what the
joy of the saints means. . . . And why so much
preaching is lost among us, and professors run
from sermon to sermon and are never weary of
hearing or reading and yet have such languishing
and starved souls; I know no truer or greater cause
than their ignorance and unconscionable neglect
of contemplation.'

Richard Baxter

'Today is the first day of the rest of your life'
*Anonymous chalk inscription on the Pitt Press
Building, Cambridge—since erased.*

THE RECIPE FOR MAKING THEOLOGY IS SIMPLE : GOD AND
man. A theologian is nothing more nor less than a person
who is interested in those two beings and how they
belong together. Just as the recipe is simple, so will be
the serving of the final dish; but life in the kitchen is
very different. It is a continual crisis which makes cooks
at work notoriously touchy people. Things can easily
go wrong : a lack of balance in the flavours, faulty
timing, and the whole thing is spoiled. In moderately

well-to-do houses of the old days all this was kept well out of sight. The lady of the house would summon cook and establish the week's menus. Dishes would then arrive at the table, cooked in the manner to which the family was accustomed. All that has changed now. In the first place, some skill in cooking, or at least in helping with it, is required of most of us. No longer are we strangers to the kitchen. In the second place the tradition is not as definite as it used to be. Holidays abroad have given people a taste for outlandish dishes just as the Indian Empire once gave Englishmen a liking for curry. What we eat and how to prepare it has become everybody's business and, at the same time, much more varied.

This is a parable of the present situation in theology. Once upon a time the theologian could work away in the isolation of the study and serve up good traditional doctrine to a believing public which knew what it liked or had to like what it got. Now it is different. Books like John Robinson's *Honest to God* and (more impressively) Dietrich Bonhoeffer's *Letters and Papers from Prison* have broken down the dividing wall and opened to a startled public the view of a theologian at work, wrestling with difficulties, wondering, exploring, getting things wrong and getting things right. It is like those contemporary restaurants where a plate-glass window allows the public to see into the kitchen. Our situation is similar but more radical. If a believing person is to survive nowadays he must get into the kitchen himself and share the difficulties and the triumphs which used to belong to the professionals alone. This book is meant as an elementary guide to coping with this revolution. Theology is too important to be left to the theologians. Since also, as with food, a greater range and a wider experience is now required it will draw on areas outside those which have usually been thought of as religious and theological. It is an introduction to living off the country for those who can no longer afford to live off other people's expertise, do not want to live out of tins and are ready to try new ways as well as old.

The task is to explore some of the points at which God and man meet. There is that fundamental simplicity about it. There is plenty of material, but it is difficult to handle. God and man are not beings which can be defined once and for all at the outset and thereafter used as counters in a problem-solving game until the right arrangement gives the right answer. They tease and refuse to be caught. It would of course be convenient if we could begin by clearing up the nature of God and the nature of man and then move on to solve the problems posed by their belonging-together. But if that were possible the whole theological enterprise could have been successfully wound up years ago. It is not possible because the material does not consist of problems but of something bigger—mysteries. The difference has been clearly expressed by Hugh Maycock. 'Problems can be solved and are all in the end soluble once one has found through research the right technique. But a mystery cannot be solved in this way because we are ourselves part of it. It is a problem—but a problem which withstands exhaustive analysis for it encroaches on its own data. We are involved in it and are part of it. We cannot place ourselves outside it, we are inside it. I do not comprehend it. It comprehends me. . . . It is not a problem I can solve by finding the right technique. I am part of it and it is only by living in it that truthful insight comes.' This is one reason why people inside the churches and outside them refuse to deal with the mystery at the heart of things and even deny its existence. Its refusal to be defined and made cashable is answered by their impatience, fear and neglect. They pretend it is not there. That is a foolish reaction for, whether we like it or not, the mystery is still there, transcending even orthodoxy, and at any time the accidents of life and death can bring it home to us with alarming force. Then the armour in which we trusted, our ability to solve problems, will be woefully inadequate. It is wiser to get on speaking terms with it before that happens by taking up the task of prayer and theology. The mystery will still come as a shock to our attitudes and opinions. It always does. Coping with it will still be testing and strenuous. Joseph Conrad's *Typhoon* and a host of other novels and plays confirm our intuition that the measure of a man's character is his ability to tolerate it, deal with it, and stand it. It takes everything he has and more. The sensible course is to begin to understand a little more about it now : not by making theories which the wind will blow away but by a close and honest attention to our own experience, since the only positions which really count or are tenable are the ones of which we say 'here I stand, I can no other'. Final understanding and definition will always elude us, but some understanding and some definition are essential, if only as a firm foothold for reaching more.

* * *

The two poles between which the investigation will move can be given many names: the familiar and the new, the given and the sought, something understood and something baffling. Some of the recognised experts are very tough about which is the correct point of departure. Karl Barth, writing about prayer, asserts that 'we shall not begin with an account of what a man does when he prays. Certainly he does something, he acts; but to understand that action we must begin at the end, that is to say, consider in the first place the answering of prayer.' Yet when he insists that 'God is not without man' he is stating the belonging-together of the two from which it must follow that if we start exploring with man we may come to God—if we are looking for him. The story of Barth's own thinking went the other way, starting with the otherness of God and ending with his humanity. We shall begin with an account of what a man does when he prays. This has the advantage that, for all its mystery, most of us have been forced to reflect on what it means to be human and made a modest collection of insights about it. God, after all, can look after himself. Our constant attention, defence or proclamation is not necessary to him. He will still be there. 'God is his own interpreter and he will make it plain.' In the end we have no more chance of escaping him than of escaping our own humanity, for man is not without God. The point can be made clearer by thinking about what happens when a work of art interests someone.

In the first instance the story begins with the individual, me. I am filling up time in the lunch hour by walking round a gallery. It might be the trivial accident of tired feet which makes me sit down in front of one particular picture which is opposite a sofa. Then I find that it has begun to arouse my interest, no doubt because a crowd of past experiences have nudged me towards a point of view which is within reach of the point of view from which the painter worked : I have walked in countryside and light like that, grown those flowers, known something of the suffering on that face. But I have been careful to say that my point of view is somewhere near the artist's and not precisely the same. They are different points, connected by a community of interest. The more I look at the picture the clearer this becomes. Here is something given, something so entirely itself that I will never be able to pin it down or possess it. In an idle moment I thought I would explore it. Now I find that it is exploring me. It takes over the primacy and the initiative, making me remember that it was there long before I came across it—perhaps unregarded in an attic before an expert discovered it. There was a beginning before my beginning, and Barth's emphasis was right. Yet all the time it was waiting for my discovery. I leave the gallery telling myself that I must find out more about the picture and the man who made it, wanting to learn about someone other than me who lived at another time and in another place. There are differences of outlook and circumstances which I must, with the help of art critics and historians, come to appreciate. Yet my incentive for that is not academic. I sense that there is something in this for me and hope to discover that community of interest which does not blur differences and makes life worth living.

Hans Urs von Balthasar says that 'just as in love I encounter the other as the other in all his freedom, and am confronted by something which I cannot dominate in any sense, so in the aesthetic sphere it is impossible to attribute the form which presents itself to a fiction of my imagination. In both cases the 'understanding' of that which reveals itself cannot be subsumed under categories which imply control.' The experience of love is parallel to that of painting and more universal. Someone is attracted to another because of a host of circumstantial accidents: the fact that they both got into a railway carriage on a wet day or are both interested in tennis or are both disappointed. This can go on to disclose a community of interest deeper than hobbies or coincidences which brings with it the temptation to make the other person a hook onto which one hangs all one's dreams and fantasies. That is corrected by the realisation that here is someone different with another story, someone who is simply there and has to be studied and learned for his own sake. The learning will be undertaken gladly because of the conviction that 'there's something in it for me'. The whole relationship will develop in terms of those two poles of difference and community. Augustine found the same thing when in his *Confessions* he pondered the story of his discovery of God. It was really God's discovery of him—a God who was his though certainly not him. 'I have come to know you so late, beauty so old and so new!'

We are dealing with a meeting between what is simply and freely *there* and our own experience. Fundamentally we are investigating the encounter of God and man, but will try to do so in a way which will 'show how religious language can gear into other language and lay bare the points of intersection' (Bernard Williams), and begin by looking at a poet at work. In his task of trying to say something about mystery he is the theologian's ally.

Some time before he was executed for losing a battle in AD 303 the Chinese poet and general Lu Chi wrote a Fu, which means an extended meditation on the poet's trade or art. This, in the discreet rhetoric of his time, is a little of what he says about himself:

Taking his position at the hub of things he contemplates the mystery of the universe;
He feeds his mind and his emotions on the great works
of the past.
Moving along with the four seasons, he sighs at the
passing of time.
Gazing at the myriad objects, he thinks of the com-
plexity of the world.

The opening words: 'taking his position at the hub of
things, he contemplates . . .' give a picture or diagram
of spokes converging on a particular point, and that
point is occupied by an individual human being with
the capacity of observing, thinking and feeling. It all
comes together in him, including the past and (because
he is human) the continual trickling away of time. The
idea is put with particular happiness at the centre of
Thomas Traherne's theology: 'Such endless depths lie
in the divinity and wisdom of God that as he maketh one,
so he maketh everyone, the end of the world, the super-
numerary persons being enrichers of his inheritance . . .
so that I alone am the centre of the world, angels and men
being all mine.' But we would be wrong if we were to take
this in a vague and general way. We must notice that there
is something quite deliberate and explicit in it. It is a disciplined matter of putting oneself at the centre of receptivity
in order to 'take things in'. People who pray, with their
daily discipline, have to be equally deliberate, equally
explicit. For they have a similar end in view, to

take upon us the mystery of things
As if we were God's spies.

Having done that, the most trivial things can be seen in a new and proper light.

The same notion of studied receptivity comes up again in a famous letter of John Keats : 'At once it struck me what quality went to make a man of achievement, and which Shakespeare possessed so enormously—I mean negative capability, that is when a man is capable of being in uncertainties, mysteries, doubts, without any irritable reaching after fact and reason.' Negative capability is a puzzling phrase, but its meaning can be filled out and clarified by calling in a later and more theological writer, Simone Weil. Her remarkable essay 'Reflections on the Right Use of School Studies' is the best possible introduction to contemplation. She says : 'Most often, attention is confused with a kind of muscular effort. If one says to one's pupils "Now you must pay attention" one sees them contracting their brows, holding their breath, stiffening their muscles. If after two minutes they are asked what they have been paying attention to, they cannot reply. They have been concentrating on nothing. They have not been paying attention. They have been contracting their muscles.'

True attention, on the other hand, 'consists of suspending our thought, leaving it detached, empty and ready to be penetrated by the object; it means holding in our minds, within reach of this thought but on a lower level

and not in contact with it, the diverse knowledge we
have acquired which we are forced to make use of. . . .
Above all our thought should be empty, waiting, not
seeking anything, but ready to receive in its naked truth
the object which is to penetrate it.' This could be put in
another way by saying that the important rule is to
observe the distance and the difference, distinct but not
insurmountable, between ourselves and the object we are
contemplating. It is as essential to communication and
seeing as it is to good manners. We need to be in less of
a hurry to write our names all over things.

There is further description of this kind of disciplined
and attentive passivity in the third section of T. S. Eliot's
East Coker.

Wait without thought, for you are not ready for
    thought

and:

In order to arrive at what you do not know
You must go by a way which is the way of ignorance.

Or there is C. Day Lewis's book of criticism *The Poetic
Image* where the poet is likened to a fisherman 'brooding
in a trance-like pose over his lines and the sea into which
they disappear. . . . Nothing he can do will compel the
fish to take his bait. He must just wait patiently'. All he
can do is to ensure that the bait is as appropriate as

possible to the ecology of the water. He will use baits which have been successful on previous occasions, but he is also ready to try one that he has not used before. It is a nice combination of luck and sympathetic judgment. The most unlikely baits have brought in some of the biggest fish—but usually to skilled and seasoned anglers.

A masterly, and more explicitly theological evaluation of contemplation is to be found in von Balthasar's *Prayer*. For him, negative capability is the way to hear and receive obediently (which surely includes sensitivity and appreciation) the word of God. 'Man is the being created as the hearer of the Word, and only in responding to the Word rises to his full dignity.' In another passage he is distinctly reminiscent of Lu Chi while opening up a specifically Christian dimension: 'He (the Christian) should, in thought and imagination, put himself in the place and situation where the word of God sounds audibly and impinges on the senses, and taking his stand there let a real and concrete meeting with God build itself up by degrees'—which seems to make church-going an obvious, though not exclusive, possibility. At the centre of Balthasar's work, combining protestant doctrine and catholic imagery, is the classic picture of reception, Mary at the annunciation: 'Behold I am the handmaid of the Lord, be it unto me according to your word.'

This phrase 'the Word of God' is always puzzling, for it covers a very wide frame of reference, with the words of scripture at one end, and at the other something much more mysterious, something to do with a sense of being stopped in one's tracks by an objective call from outside, from some independent centre of existence. Yet it strikes into the subjective 'me' with disturbing force, either fearful or happy. I am surprised by joy—or by something less agreeable. In the Biblical tradition the Word interrupts chaos at the beginning and calls something new into being, in the threat and promise of a prophet it calls for a change of heart and mind, in the interpretation of Christ the New Testament writers seize on it. The combination of otherness ('from without') and likeness ('within'), the heavenly man who becomes flesh in Pauline and Johannine theology, leads to the identification of Jesus with the word of God. He brings a judgment and a promise both of which are beyond our expectations and in that sense uncalled for. But once brought they require some kind of response. They call us. Without something like this contemplation would become a very stuffy business and lapse into a self-indulgent and sub-poetic vein. We would, as Barth warns, be going round and round like squirrels in a cage.

But this 'word of God' talk is so gigantic and majestic that we need something more humdrum and manageable to act as an equivalent for it. This can be done by the phrase 'circumstances beyond our control'. Whatever these may be, love, death or the more trivial interruptions of our existence, our contemplation must be

open to them and wrestle with them if it is to keep
healthy and alive. This means that it will be under constant pressure, the garden of the soul opening out to the
street and getting trampled and disordered in consequence. That is the threat. But there is a promise too.
We surely want something better than heightened sensitivity for ourselves; we are surely after something other
than that—both in a workaday and a theological sense.
This is recognition, a word which stands for our central
concern, the intersection of the 'I' and something else,
a meeting which confirms both of these poles without
confusing them.

It is something that we all want very much because
it has the possibility of making us happy. It is a category
of relationship, not possible outside the conjunction of
an 'I' and a 'Thou', and reaches its perfection when it
is mutual : the blessed state of affairs which St Paul
looks forward to when he says 'then shall I know even as
I am known'. In other words, although the divine recognition of him is complete his knowledge of God is only
partial, so the fulfilment is still to come. The most
familiar example of it is when somebody, loaded with
perplexities or half-grasped ideas, tells them to somebody
else; and that someone, after listening, says something
which gathers it all together, so making a piece of solid
ground and opening a way forward. What is said may
be as banal as 'Where there's a will there's a way' or
'God loves you', but it is felt as new and helpful. The
most far-reaching instance is when somebody recognises

another for what he is, a combination a full knowledge and full acceptance, and this is returned. That is recognition under its highest form of love. In the measure in which we have had it we are able to live. A person does not know who he is, certainly does not dare to go ahead and be it, unless another person brings it out. Then it will have validity apart from himself. There will be that distance which allows free action. To put it in an awkward sentence, he will have been made objective to himself.

This business of objectifying is the stock in trade of doctors, counsellors and psychiatrists. It is also the occupation of the poet who tries to bring things to recognition by drawing them into the light and giving them names so that we in turn can respond to them as we could not, or dared not, do before. In his essay *Priest and Poet* Karl Rahner discusses the word as a sacrament, 'the corporeal state in which what we now experience and think first begins to exist by fashioning itself into this its word-body'.

In Christian doctrine the word which is very near us, which is on our lips and in our hearts, which is ours, becomes objective in Christ in a way which allows the to and the fro of dialogue. A 'Thou' is established over against the 'I', and the 'I' is thereby enhanced and liberated.

We can see the function of words as effective means of recognition in some lines of Rilke :

Sind wir vielleicht hier, um zu sagen : Haus,
Brücke, Brunnen, Tor, Krug, Obstbaum, Fenster,
Höchstens : Säule, Turm . . . aber zu sagen versteh's
O zu sagen so wie selber die Dinge niemals
innig meinten zu sein.
(Are we, perhaps, here, in order to say : House,
Bridge, fountain, gate, urn, fruit tree, window,
At the highest : pillar, tower . . . but to say it, please
  understand,
O to say what the things themselves in themselves
  never thought to be.)

There might be a recollection here of Genesis 2.19 : 'So
out of the ground the Lord God formed every beast of
the field and every bird of the air, and brought them to
man to see what he would call them; and whatever the
man called every living creature, that was its name.'
Adam in paradise lived in the state towards which our
prayers only strive, undamaged communion with God.
So this humdrum activity of saying 'giraffe, horse,
sparrow, magpie' was part of that worship. God's evoca-
tion of the creatures into being is followed by man doing
something very similar with his words. The charming
way in which God stands back to see what man would
call them might even lead us to say that God has given
us language in order to share with us the dignity of
revealing what things are. We do not always make a
good job of it. Kierkegaard has a satirical note on the
Genesis story : 'the first book of Moses cites as one of

the distinctive marks of man : to give animals names. Now it is characteristic of the ordinary man, the man of the people, to have that gift. If the ordinary man sees a bird for some years which is not usually seen, he immediately gives it a name. But take ten learned men and how incapable they are of finding a name. What a satire on them that when one reads scientific works and sees the names which come from the people, and then the silly miserable names when once in a while a learned man has to think of a name. Usually they can think of nothing better than calling the animal or the plant after their own names.' Good names and good language evoke something of the nature of the thing itself, its individuality and difference. They assist in the mysterious process of creation which Rahner describes by saying that 'all realities sigh for their own unveiling. They want themselves to enter, if not as knowers at least as objects of knowledge, into the light and knowledge of love. They all have a dynamic drive to fulfil themselves by being known.'

Contemplation, then, means seeing what is going on. To pray is deliberately to take time to remember and look and let things speak to us. We hold them in our hands and turn them over. More than this, it is something like a calling of things out of chaos into distinct being—which is what is meant by the word 'body'. We become a point of rest and recognition; also we are doing something creative.

So W. H. Auden pictures the dying Sigmund Freud :

> he closed his eyes
> upon that last picture common to us all,
> of problems like relatives gathered
> puzzled and jealous about our dying.

> For about him to the very end were still
> those he had studied, the fauna of the night,
> and shades that still waited to enter
> the bright circle of his recognition.

We are left to carry on what Freud started. Particularly we are 'to be enthusiastic over the night', not only because of its mystery but also

> because it needs our love. With large sad eyes
> its delectable creatures look up and beg
> us dumbly to ask them to follow.
> they are exiles who long for the future

> that lies in our power, they too would rejoice
> if allowed to serve enlightenment like him.

This coincides with a basic Biblical pattern. In the bible certain events in the course of time are seen as normative, revealing what was going on before and illuminating the future. For the Jews in exile the remembered story of the Exodus, meeting with Babylonian myth, gave rise to the vision of a similar exodus of the world out of nothingness into being. It gave a hope for the future—recreation and freedom : 'Thus says the Lord

God : Behold I will open your graves, O my people, and I will bring you home into the land of Israel.' Similarly in the New Testament, the gospel of Jesus Christ draws on a new understanding of tradition and is a revival of future hope. It could not be put more simply than in the Christmas hymn :

> The hopes and fears of all the years
> Are met in thee tonight.

To recognise things or people by means of words has both a passive and an active aspect. It is like the purposive passivity of Day Lewis's fisherman. We are passive in that we let things speak to us in their own way, active in that by doing so we call them into the light and into individual existence. This is probably why young children are fascinated with the names of things. Every child, and every adult too, has some words that are particularly important to him because of their associations. They evoke a crowd of recollections. Freud pointed out that we have a way of forgetting some words because of the intolerable or unresolved memories which they would call to mind. Others are treasured because they give pleasure. As the great Citizen Kane dies in Orson Welles's film he utters a single word 'Rosebud'. When his property burns at the end of his story we catch a glimpse of the same word on a child's sledge. For people in love it is the name of the beloved. This is very delicately expressed in a poem from Paul

B

Verlaine's *La Bonne Chanson*. He assembles the things which the name of his beloved brings to mind and only at the end mentions that name:

> Une sainte en son aureole,
> Une châtelaine en sa tour,
> Tout ce que contient la parole
> Humaine de grace et d'amour.

More images and memories follow, and he ends:

> Je vois, j'entends toutes ces choses
> ~~Dans son nom Carlovingein.~~

In praying nothing matters so much as the name of God 'I am who I am—I am with you'—that name which points to the utterly free by refusing an ordinary name which would limit it, and yet promises a continual and unbreakable relationship. It points to faithfulness and freedom, and for the devout man it recalls occasions when that faithfulness and freedom have become actual in his experience or the experience of the community to which he belongs.

All this demands a certain discipline. The key-word here is 'resistance'. There was a deliberateness about Lu Chi taking his position at the hub of things. There was a note of defiance in Keats's refusal of 'any irritable reaching after fact and reason'. Simone Weil, in the essay referred to earlier, has this to say: 'All wrong translations, all absurdities in geometry problems, all clumsiness of style and all faulty connection of ideas in composi- tions and essays, all such things are due to the fact that thought has seized upon some idea too hastily, and being thus prematurely blocked, is not open to the truth.'

There is a common temptation, which crops up as obstinately in social as it does in religious circles, to pretend to insights, virtues or knowledge which we have not really made our own. To succumb to it is to lose before we start. The word of God addresses a man where he is, so he gains nothing by putting himself somewhere else, though only in wish or imagination. If he does so in order to avoid the disturbance and judgment of that word, then he will, by cocooning himself in a dishonest muddle, miss its comfort too because the two are bound up together indissolubly.

This needs some qualification, because there can be no doubt that in prayer and liturgy we do have recourse to language and sentiments that are more exalted than usual. Like the best theology and the best art it contains an element of exaggeration which catches our attention and draws us further on than we usually go. That is good and useful, and not many people would care to live without some kind of 'heightening' of this kind. But it must always be checked against the drab or brutal facts of our existence. It may sound banal, but to avoid being somewhere else, to avoid being someone else, requires a determined act of resistance. We need to attend to the apostolic injunction 'Stand firm'.

Because of this there will always be ambiguity in the Christian attitude to the world. Theologians who tell us to get involved will always be answered, with more or less sense, by theologians telling us to 'come out of her, my people'. It is there in St John's gospel, it is there in St Paul's letter to the Romans if you compare the first two chapters with the eighth. God loves the world, and this is evident because in Christ he is both present in it and working out its salvation to a fuller life. It is evident in the insistence on the body and flesh of Jesus. But also, God in Christ is against the world. It is resisted, judged and overcome, not out of mere bloody-mindedness but in order that it may receive a peace and kingdom which are not its own and which it could never make out of its own resources. And this is evident in the insistence on spirit as against flesh, death and the second birth.

There is a parable of it in the working of any creative artist, thinker, scientist or lover. These people are *contra mundum*. They separate themselves from ordinary distraction, sometimes to the point of eccentricity. They are called absent-minded, but this is only a hostile way of describing their extraordinary present-mindedness, for they do this in order to be present with some particular point in the world and to know it: the artist and lover with a particular human face for instance; the scientist with a particular cell or organism. The resistance is in the service of recognising.

Prayer, being a similar quest for recognition, is a

imilarly aggressive act. R. D. Laing's polemical *Politics of Experience* amounts to a defence of the individual's internal experience against the external pressures of pseudo-orthodoxy and 'the alienated starting point of our pseudo-sanity'. Laing pins his faith on a man like his patient Jesse Watkins going on his journey into the interior : 'Yes, the—that was the enormity of it, that I— that there was no way of avoiding this—facing up to what I—the journey I had to do.' The journey meant taking on the 'enormity of knowing' and ended in a return to a world where 'the grass was greener, the sun was shining brighter, and people were more alive, I could see them clearer'. The man of prayer also is marked by some of the refusal to be put off of Bunyan's Christian, some of the gay abandon of Edward Lear's Jumblies :

> They went to sea in a sieve they did
>   In a sieve they went to sea :
> In spite of all their friends could say
> On a winter's morn, on a stormy day
>   In a sieve they went to sea !
>
> And everyone said who saw them go
> 'O won't they soon be upset you know !
> For the sky is dark and the voyage is long
> And, happen what may, it's extremely wrong
>   In a sieve to sail so fast'

In the face of prudent warnings and respectable advice :

They called aloud 'Our sieve ain't big,
But we don't care a button, we don't care a fig,
In a sieve we'll go to sea !'

The incentive for this daunting journey is the possibilit
or promise of finding 'a land all covered with trees
furnished with useful and delightful commodities, wha
Herbert calls 'the land of spices', and of returnin
mysteriously taller from

the lakes and the terrible zone
And the hills of the Chankley Bore.

CHAPTER TWO

The Old Curiosity Shop

'I was so ignorant that I did not think that any man in the world had had such thoughts before. Seeing them therefore so amiable, I wondered not a little that nothing was spoken of them in former ages: but as I read the Bible I was here and there surprised with such thoughts, and found by degrees that these things had been written of before, not only in the scriptures, but in many of the fathers and this was the way of communion with God in all saints, as I saw clearly in the person of David. Methoughts a new light darted into all his psalms, and finally spread abroad over the whole Bible, so that things which for their obscurity I thought not in being were contained, things which for their greatness were incredible were made evident, and things obscure, plain: God by this means bringing me into the very heart of his kingdom.'

Traherne

'How was it that I recognised them when they were mentioned and agreed that they were true? It must have been that they were already in my memory, hidden away in its deepest recesses, in so remote a part of it that I might not have been able to think of them at all, if some other person had not brought them to the fore by teaching me about them.'

Augustine

TRADITION IS SECOND-HAND BY DEFINITION. IT CONSISTS of a variety of doctrines, proverbs, precepts, stories and rituals which are handed down from generation to generation. That is what makes it unappetising. People can be as reluctant to take on other people's spiritual and moral paraphernalia as younger sisters are to be dressed in their older sister's clothes. They prefer something which is more themselves: something more like the first-hand insights of the last chapter. At the same time it does not seem possible for people to be entirely happy without a tradition. If the contemporary student throws out the values of his parents it is only to pick up the values of William Blake, Maoist China or the travellers of the American West. Pastiche and nostalgia are stocks-in-trade of the modern cinema. In the early days of Stowe School a notice appeared on the board which began with the words 'From tomorrow the tradition of the school will be . . .' Anyone who enters into theology and prayer is immediately confronted with a mound of traditional stuff. How is he to sort it out in a way which does justice to his creative chariness about taking on second-hand material and to his creative need of a tradition of some kind? It can be done, as the work of any great artist or scientist makes clear. He draws on the past but has an unmistakable individual voice. The question is—how?

The quickest guide is to think of a great depository of tradition, like the Christian Church, as a junk-shop. It is as foolish to pass it by as to buy up its entire contents. There is a good chance that amongst the clutter there will be something useful or beautiful, something that, with a little adaptation or cleaning, we can make our own. That chance is missed by the people who insist that everything about them should be new and should have had as little previous history as possible before it became theirs. They do not only miss the opportunity of saving a little money. They also exclude themselves from the lively possibility of finding the great bargain. That stroke of luck usually comes only to the seasoned and dedicated hunters because they have given time and study to the matter. They have read about porcelain or English water-colours and examined the specimens in the museum so that their practised eye soon picks out the thing of quality in the back-street shop which casual browsers have missed. In the parable it was the merchant, the professional, who spotted the pearl of great price. The incentive for taking the trouble to pick over the great deposit of Christian tradition is the likelihood that something in it will prove delightful or useful to us. The desire to be something of an expert follows naturally from this. It entails patient and objective study of the history and circumstances of the chosen field in the tradition and it holds the promise of making a discovery which could enrich and clarify the minds and attitudes of more people than the discoverer alone.

Nowhere is the detached and dedicated study demanded of the expert more important than in the attempt to understand tradition in a way which brings it alive. The basic technique is the same, and as simple, as that described in the previous chapter. It is a matter of looking at something for its own sake instead of pushing and wrenching it to suit our present opinions of how things should be : a discipline of letting it speak. If we can practise that 'negative capability' we may also be surprised at the immediate relevance of the object of our study. It may set us off on a new and better way of looking at a wide variety of things. A resounding example of this in recent writing is Peter Brown's biography of St Augustine, where a detailed knowledge of the world the man lived in serves to bring him alive in a way which makes him contemporary. Similar efforts are being made with the books of the Bible. Scholars are labouring to recover the circumstances of the writers, the interests which motivated them and the influences which shaped them. Much of it is incomprehensible or irrelevant to the general reader, but in the hands of a master it can have the effect of removing the varnish and the over-painting of the ages to reveal something illuminating and new.

Traditional statements about God are dry and dusty. There are so many of them that selection is difficult, even if they looked appetising enough for us to take the pains. A significant part of the trouble is that they have got isolated into one great cluttered heap, just as the pictures which once occupied positions of importance in homes or churches have been crowded into wearisome museums. They have been removed from their proper place. We need to get them back into it in order to revive them and appreciate them, for they meant something there which they can never mean elsewhere.

Statements about God which now look so dull were once wrung out of perplexity and doubt so that they came as new revelations. They were immediate in a way which is best described in Karl Barth's words about genuine theology: 'All human thought and speech in relation to God can have only the character of response to be made to God's word. Human thought and speech cannot be about God but must be directed towards God, called into action by the divine thought and speech directed to men, and following and corresponding to this work of God. . . . What is essential to human language is to speak of man in the first person (I) and of God in the second person (thou). And this means that theological work must really and truly take place in the form of a liturgical act, as invocation of God and as prayer.' And again: 'Theological work does not merely begin with prayer, and is not merely accompanied by it; in its totality it is peculiar to and characteristic of theology that it can only be done in the act of prayer.' That is to say that theology is not an idle thought-game but can only be done by particular people who are prepared to stand up to the central mystery and face it out. Jacob became a theologian when he spent the night wrestling with a stranger and would not let him go until he blessed him. He limped off into the dawn with a new name, the name which every theologian should want, 'Israel—

for you have striven with God and with man and have prevailed.' It became the name of a nation. Job became a theologian when he refused the second-hand rational-isations of his advisers, insisting on his own integrity and an answer from God. Then he saw for himself and became the one who could offer sacrifice and prayer for his foolish friends. The man who has struggled with humanity and divinity becomes the focus of revelation and of community. His theology is the only sort which need interest anybody.

In referring to Jacob and Job we have been drawing on tradition in the form of stories. The point is worth dwelling on and thinking about.

The virtue of a story is that it does the very thing we are looking for. We see statements and convictions aris-ing within the contradictions of human experience. We are told how they come about. They have a particular situation and they belong to it so inextricably that they cannot be cut out of it, the 'meaning' or 'message' lifted out and the story then thrown away. We have to take the thing whole. The story must be told again, not reduced to an abstract generalisation. And we listen eagerly. Why?

Stories show us our way about. They indicate some of the possibilities of life and some of its limitations.

Somebody may say 'forgive your enemies' or 'honesty is the best policy' but can I? and is it? The answer is the story of someone who forgave his enemies so we can see how it is done and what happens when we do it.

Here is the tale of a man who always believed and said that honesty is the best policy so we can assess for ourselves whether this way of thinking is a good bet or not. When we read a biography or a novel, or see a film, we will, if it is any good, recognise in one of the characters at least concerns which are also ours. We will identify with him. Having done that, having put ourselves beside one of the characters or got into his skin because of this kinship of interest, then we are on tenterhooks to find out how things might turn out for him. Will he make it or will he crumble? How did he make it if he did, or what was fatal when he collapsed? For those in love then, going to see *Romeo and Juliet* or *Cosi Fan Tutte* or reading about Abelard and Heloise will be an intense and engrossing experience. For those in authority *King Lear* will have an extraordinary potency. But whether we are old or young, in love or out, there are questions which we all share. What shall I do with my hopes—live on them, forget them or adapt them? Is there any chance of my hunger for love and understanding being satisfied? What *am* I to do about my parents?

Any good answer to questions like these will have something of the story about it. It could be personal and conversational : 'I had that problem too, and with me it worked itself out like this . . .' or we could ask the questioner to tell his own story, illuminating the question and even beginning to answer it by narrating the way in which it has come to be asked. Or we could say 'You should meet X. He knows about this sort of thing'—

meaning that he knows about it in his own experience
and biography. This is a good answer in the sense that
we will find here something which we can use, something
which we can make our own. This other story will clarify
our own, by its likeness to it and its differences from it.
If it all boils down to a principle, 'where there's a will
there's a way' or 'God is love', then that principle will
have the solidity and shape of something which we have
seen happening, growing under stress and sunshine. It
will no longer be cloudy. It will have become incarnate
and had a history. To see something in its setting is the
only way of really seeing anything. And seeing it in one
setting we can take it into our own setting. It can come
home to us, for old pictures can be revived by taking
them home as well as by restoring them to their original
place. A story is both a direct and indirect means of
communication and so both satisfying and teasing. It is
direct in the sense that it overcomes the incurably
abstract remoteness of precepts and ideas. In the story
it is concrete and it happens. That is satisfying. At the
same time it is removed from me precisely because of
this. The story will always be about someone who is
rather different from me and set in more or less different
circumstances. This teases me out of myself and leads me
on into something other than myself which I will never
be able to master or overcome entirely. In some way it
will always elude me. This makes my relationship with
it decidedly ambiguous, and rather like my relationship
with someone I love—mine own yet not mine own, for

me, yet having a life of its own. The most satisfying answer is also the most teasing.

And this is the kind of answer that Christianity gives. In the end all that it has to tell is a story, and all that it has to tell is in that story. It is told over and over again. At every service of Mass its spare and monumental outlines are present in the prayer of consecration and in what is done with the bread and wine which represent God's way with man, focussed on Jesus. Here is a life which is taken, and we recall his acceptance of life, both of earthly life in which, the story goes, he accepted gladly publicans and sinners, the ways of religious tradition and ordinary commerce, business and relationships: and in which he accepted the call of God to obey him and walk in his ways. Here is a life which is broken in a death brought about both by the ordinary mechanisms of political expediency and by the will of God. Here is a life which is given—given to us by the man for others and given to God by the man for God, and so raised up into a new life beyond the breaking. Here is one who not only said that whoever seeks his life must lose it, but one to whom this actually happened. Here is the story of a wrestling with humanity and divinity, the ordinary and the mysterious.

All that I have said previously about stories applies here. We are given a sense of the possibilities of our own lives. A theology which, in other hands, could easily degenerate into an idea, is embodied and incarnate. In the story which the apostles told and which is still the centre of the church we have something which satisfies by being ours and teases by not being ours. It is a story which is always there for us but which we have never finished with, and so it is told again and again and each time we lay our own lives and stories alongside it.

So the story is repeated, and the creed has the form of a recital which marks it off from more generalised forms such as declarations of the rights of man or the sonorous prologue to the American constitution. What determines and invigorates a community, it seems, is not a collection of ideals but a common story. Perhaps we have seen something of this in the recent re-telling of the histories of the first World War or the Battle of Britain. In political motivation stories like the Battle of the Boyne have a particularity which is easier to identify with than the moral precepts of the politicians. In a similar way the story of Christ ('Tell me the old, old story') has played a determinative role in Christian tradition over and above doctrinal formulations. This set in at the earliest possible stage.

In the earliest Christian writings that have survived, Paul's letters, he tells us that the way in which he proclaimed his belief was by telling the story of Jesus's death and resurrection. He did not do this by way of entertaining his listeners with an amazing and curious tale. Christ died 'for our sins' and rose 'according to the scriptures'. Whatever else that may mean it implies that we are implicated in the story and so is God, the subject of the scriptures. Every page of Paul makes it clear that

his tale has such immediate implications that he expects
something of it to take place in the living experience of
his readers. This is their death, their resurrection. They
must understand their lives in terms of it. In the next
Christian generation a man called Mark took the bold
and creative step of presenting the whole thing in a
narrative form which bound together the living concerns
of a group of bewildered and persecuted believers with
traditions about the life of their master. Matthew then
made this story of Mark's the line onto which he pegged
a wealth of ethical instruction—to its great benefit in
interest and immediacy. Luke capped them both in a
work which contains most of the best Christian stories
(the Christmas tales, the prodigal son, the good
Samaritan and the walk to Emmaus). It is done with a
much greater narrative skill and charm than Mark could
manage and the ethics have a secular common-sense
which makes them more universal than in Matthew
where they are basically ecclesiastical. In Ezra Pound's
classification, Mark is the inventor who does a new thing
in a rough fashion, Matthew and Luke the masters who
exploit and perfect it. John stands apart from these three,
yet wrote a book in which doctrinal discourses alternate
with dramatic scenes and each illuminates the other.
The significant fact is that Christianity became most
itself in telling a story which could be told and told
again, with differences of emphasis and from a variety
of view-points to make it continually new. It has never
lost that character in spite of theologians who see con-

ceptual argument as their vocation rather than story-telling, and so lose the initiative to Dostoyevsky and David Kossoff. Stories can be the best theology because in them we can see things happen in a way which defies abstraction. They make it both immediate and distant. By being ours and not ours they contain the two poles of the investigation, likeness and unlikeness, clarity and mystery. By being themselves they interest us.

The poet Edwin Muir in his autobiography saw his own life as a narrative on the two levels of individual difference and shared mystery, calling them story and fable. Story refers to a man's biography where fact is linked to fact: birth and parents, changes of address, marriage and jobs. It marks him off from other people. It is his alone. But the fable is always impinging on it. This is the chain of images and archetypes which we do not entirely understand and which only become clear in dreams, visions and myths: the country of innocence, the fall, the journey and transfiguration. Thus story tells us that when the poet was a boy, the Muir family moved from a good farm on the Orkneys to a bad one and then to the urban environment of Glasgow. But what is happening in the realm of fable is a fall from innocence into experience and alienation. It is in the realm of fable that we have our deepest connections with one another. In biography we are distinct. It must be to the fable that his wife Willa refers when she says that 'he never ceased to believe that his experience resembled the experience of everyone else living on earth'. In his autobiography

Muir himself describes a time when the two realms touched, the meeting point being a thoroughly traditional form of words. His wife was very ill in hospital, and he himself in the grip of one of the depressions which plagued him. In the street he saw some boys playing the traditional game of marbles:

'the old game had come round again at its own time, known only to children, and it seemed a little rehearsal for a resurrection promising a timeless renewal of life. That night I wrote in my diary: Last night going to bed alone I suddenly found myself (I was taking off my waistcoat) reciting the Lord's prayer in a loud, emphatic voice—a thing I had not done for many years—with deep urgency and profound disturbed emotion. While I went on I grew more composed; as if I had been empty and craving were replenished, my soul grew still; every word had a strange fullness of meaning which astonished and delighted me. . . . Now I realised that, quite without knowing it, I was a Christian, no matter how bad a one . . . I did not turn to any church . . . I had no conception of the splendours of Christendom. I remained quite unaware of them until some years later I was sent by the British Council to Italy.'

Muir has given us an instance of the convergence of the individual story and the archetypal story or 'fable' in the biography of one man. To see the same thing happen on a wider plane we can turn to another traditional thing, ritual. Here the individual finds himself as a member of a crowd, or rather a community. His personal experience is linked to common experience by traditional actions, his story joined to the fable.

Monica Wilson tells us that whenever she asked the women of an African tribe why they set such store by their ceremonies of birth, maturity, marriage and death she always received the same answer. The purpose of the rites was 'to stop people going mad'. People go mad because of the dread of having to adjust to new forms of life, or having to answer alarming demands, on their own. Ritual brings the whole community in on the act; but it does so with a dignity and tact which comes from a certain detachment from the person concerned, and this is part of its strength. The ceremonies are the same whoever has come of age, got married or died. There are no alterations in the pattern for individual cases. The same old movements are gone through, the same old words recited. There is something about it which is impersonal, yet it recognises and upholds the person by breaking up the isolation which is the cause of the madness. When a man dies, his widow is first encouraged to weep and lament, then to forget and look to her new life. In these *rites de passage*, ceremonies which celebrate the transition from one kind of existence to another, the individual's predicament is confirmed. The participation of the community encourages him to bring his feelings out into the open and express them. But at

the same time the participation of the community sets
limits to these feelings and controls them, for it is possible to go mad by getting stuck in one kind of feeling as
well as by failing to express it. The two poles of ritual
are the individual and the community, personal feeling
and ancient set patterns. In this way a person's crisis of
transition is set in a strengthening time-continuum.
Looking backwards the ceremonies remind him that
these things have happened in the past, long before he
arrived on the scene. Looking forwards, he is led into a
new kind of life of which he knows little or nothing as
yet, but towards which the ceremony points inexorably.

The Christian service of the Mass or Lord's Supper *The Mass*
functions in a similar way. The participant is encouraged
by the prayers to bring out his own feelings of thanks-
giving, penitence, need or praise. In the prayer of inter-
cession he prays on behalf of statesmen, bishops, sick
people, and other matters of genuine concern to him
and the community. The old handbooks used to encour-
age the worshipper to call to mind things that he was
particularly sorry about or glad about, needs of which
he was particularly aware, though this was expected to
be done in the silence of the mind rather than out loud.
But at the centre of the service is something which
happened long before we were born, the death of Christ.
And this controls it. We may recollect, as did Dom
Gregory Dix in the last chapter of his *Shape of the
Liturgy,* the long procession of generations which have
done the same before, leading up to this moment. At

the same time as being given this reference to the past which is ours and not ours we are pointed towards a future which is to be ours yet has the same objectivity and independence of us. We 'show forth the Lord's death until he comes'. And invariably, at the centre of the service, whatever we have asked for in the prayers, whatever our state of mind or soul, we are given the same thing—bread and wine. The moment is both independent of us (it happens regardless) and intimate to us (we take it into our systems as food). It is both individual and shared. These twin aspects are necessary to a *rite de passage* which both fixes personal life and opens it up to new possibilities, history to fable, the one to the many of community, the present to the past and the future. In Christian doctrine and ritual the person of Christ is always central. He is the one who focuses and interprets the past, the one who is also the point of reference for the future which opens from him. Or again, he is both the one in whom we can recognise aspects of ourselves, and also the one who is different from us—the one among us whom we do not know.

This discussion of ritual has led us towards a realisation of the belonging-together of the immanent and the transcendent. In other words, it has led us into very deep water indeed. But it has also brought us back to the very simple fact that the Christian tradition comes to us, not as a collection of maxims or as a system of discipline, but as a story. In Christian ceremonies its recital plays a central and determinative role. This can be observed in Baptism, in the Mass, or in the spacious and evocative rites of Holy Saturday which include both of these —together with a drama of enlightenment—in a wide frame of historical and legendary reference. The story of deliverance sets the ritual pattern.

Tradition can be brought back to life in two ways. First it must be removed from the museum, the 'deposit of faith', where it suffers from being uprooted from its native soil and from being crowded with too many other objects, thus suggesting a similarity with them which can blur its individuality. It becomes a museum-piece. The restoration is done by the patient and objective researches of the scholars into its original circumstances and life-setting. If this can be achieved the second way in which tradition is revived can follow. It can come home to us as a vital and enlightening piece of life, as something useful and delightful. We live on our ability to understand other people, to lay their stories alongside our own in a community of interest which acknowledges the differences. By learning about other people and other times we get the courage and the sense to be ourselves and the bafflement of the old Socratic maxim 'know thyself' is relieved. We come to know ourselves indirectly by knowing others. To be religious is to acknowledge that one is always in the presence of the other—God. One learns about that and clarifies it by understanding other people who have made the same acknowledgment. They become allies and mentors, the detached and sympathetic appreciation of tradition offering a wide range of choice.

This variety and plurality in the tradition which research uncovers must be stoutly defended against those who want to lay an exclusive emphasis on one part of it. In Christian circles a narrow positivism about the Bible or the Eucharist (this is it, this is the thing) can impose disastrous limitations on people's capacity for exploring the mystery of humanity and divinity. Orthodoxy can be used as a heavy lid to hold down and conceal a bubbling variety of experiences. The history of Christian doctrine can be distorted by seeing it as the triumphant progress of the orthodox norm, playing down whatever does not contribute to that theme, and refusing to take anything else seriously. It was, perhaps, a sad day for Christianity when the canon of scripture was at last fixed and closed. This led the general devout public to suppose that certain books had an exceptional normative authority in the things of God and man, and still leads many scholars to study them in isolation from the life and literature they belonged to. A saying or vision of Christ in an apocryphal (i.e. uncanonical) book is all too easily dismissed as invention or fantasy while a similar thing in a New Testament gospel is all too earnestly squeezed to yield a drop of respectable fact. Within the New Testament gospels the famous search for the historical Jesus does violence to the imaginative individuality of Matthew, Mark, Luke and John. Against that should be put the psalmist's exclamation of praise,

'Lord, how manifold are thy works; in wisdom hast thou made them all'. Anyone who is worth his salt will be enthusiastic over one particular thing—this girl, this composer, this countryside or this writer. It is when this petrifies into a mannerism, an authoritarian dogma or a fanaticism, that the wise man insists that there are more things in heaven and earth—and takes his custom elsewhere. Fortunately, he can usually make his appeal to some part of the tradition which the present authorities have ignored. Primitive Christianity answered the scribal obsession with the law by rediscovering its roots in the covenant between God and man. Luther drew on Augustine and Paul for ammunition against a moribund ecclesiastical authority. The rediscovery of tradition is not the preserve of the conservatives.

Suspicion of the secondhand can easily lead to a ridiculous insistence on newness for its own sake and the neglect of valuable things simply because they are old. A credulous appetite for it can turn the living-room into a haunted and stuffy lumber-room. But for those who are prepared to select and evaluate it is a source of strength and recognition, the opening of a variety of lively and interesting views.

CHAPTER THREE

The Court of Common Pleas

'And he told them a parable, to the effect that they ought always to pray and not lose heart. He said, "In a certain city there was a judge who neither feared God nor regarded man; and there was a widow in that city who kept coming to him and saying, "Vindicate me against my adversary". For a while he refused; but afterwards he said to himself, "Though I neither fear God nor regard man, yet because this widow bothers me, I will vindicate her, or she will wear me out by her continual coming." And the Lord said, "Hear what the unrighteous judge says. And will not God vindicate his elect, who cry to him day and night? Will he delay long over them? I tell you, he will vindicate them speedily." '

Luke 18, 1-8

'Even if one did not think or suspect that the theologians in these speculations were thinking a little too much in terms of the time "Before Christ" and were not quite aware of the fact that the Word of God became flesh, and that therefore he through whom everything comes into being has become very approachable and easily moved, this in any case is true and certain: there is a prayer of petition which speaks to God and is not a mere exorcism of one's own heart, but boldly and explicitly ventures to ask him for bread, peace, restraint of his enemies, health, the spread of

his kingdom on earth, and a host of such earthly
and highly problematic things. . . . Such prayer
combines a great measure of self-will (for one
presents one's own desires) with a supreme degree
of submissiveness (for one prays to him whom
one cannot compel, persuade or charm, but only
beg).'

Karl Rahner

IS IT RUDE TO ASK? A THEOLOGICAL INVESTIGATION
which takes prayer and worship as its field bumps up
against the fact that the basic meaning of prayer is asking. If it takes the Christian tradition for its material it
is bound to unearth, sooner or later, the doctrine that
asking is the usual form of speech for a man in the
presence of God. 'Ask and you will receive' is Jesus's
word in the gospels, emphasised in Luke's by the parables
of the widow and the friend who dared to ask. 'Let your
requests be made known unto God' says Paul. We have
already heard Karl Barth insisting that genuine theological work must be praying and calling upon God.
It seems to be central, but it also seems to be the precise
point at which a great many people hand in their cards
and the theologians get into a hopeless logical muddle.
Difficult and famous questions stand in the way. If
God, as we are told, knows what we want before we ask
him, if he knows best what is good for us and will give
it to us whether we ask or not, then why ask? Then
there is the appeal to good manners. How dare we
besiege God with our impertinent requests as if we

could bludgeon him into changing his mind? Those questions have not yet received a satisfactory answer in their own terms. Probably they never will because there is a fundamental and crippling error in the terms themselves. They presuppose a certain knowledge of God, that he is omnipotent and omniscient. Taking that as a 'known', and so taking God as a 'known' they proceed to make him a counter which can be used with other counters like 'asking' (they pretend to know exactly what that is too) in a game of problems. A solution is then expected which will abolish the problem. But that is not the way to do theology. Its subject is mystery, not problems; so it works by exploring the nature of God, the nature of man and how they belong together. It does not expect to answer that question and then move on, but to ask it again and again. That is the way in which we will try to think about petition in this chapter. We will investigate it as a meeting-point of humanity and divinity. It is something which happens. If we accept that and examine it appreciatively instead of protesting from the vantage-point of superior knowledge that it should not be allowed, we may make a new discovery.

The discipline of looking discussed in the first chapter provides a way of approaching the subject of this one. 'Don't think, but look'. That maxim of Wittgenstein's asks for that suspension of thought as the prelude to proper and appropriate thinking which Keats and Simone Weil demanded. It has only to be recalled in this present context for us to realise that it is a form of asking. Contemporary theologians would call it openness to being. The looker stands empty-handed, inviting the thing or person looked at to come out and be itself. It could be called interrogatory thinking and makes us notice that asking has a respectable intellectual history before it comes to petitionary prayer, which many people do not think respectable. This provides a foothold and a way of approach for dealing with the difficulty.

Someone I love is in trouble. Should I pray for him to get better? A sophisticated and somewhat patronising answer is that it can do no harm. It will calm me down and so, as a by-product, make me more comforting and reassuring in my dealings with my afflicted friend. That avoids the difficulty of suggesting that my prayer could make any real or mysterious difference, but it does so at the cost of saying anything at all vital or interesting about people or God. A double whisky might serve as well. It has also swept the whole question of asking under the carpet by substituting recollection in tranquillity, which is a different matter. This can be made more theological by making submission to God the object of the recollection. D. Z. Phillips, a contemporary philosopher of religion, says that 'the prayer of petition is best understood, not as an attempt at influencing the way things go, but as an expression of, and as a request for, devotion to God through the way things go'. This kind of enlightened view is sure to command respect. Devotion to God in adverse circumstances is a saintly heroism

which one can only admire. But when this has become a
rule and a generalisation to cover the whole matter we
cannot feel entirely satisfied. By being in too much of a
hurry it has failed to take asking seriously. It is not so
much that it is wrong as that it wants to be right too
quickly, which is much the same thing. 'Thy will be
done' is right in the end, but before it can mean anything in a particular situation something like the preced-
ing words have to be said, and they are a request:
'Father, if it be possible, let this cup pass from me'.
Without that, the neat and respectable answer is bought
at the price of boring divinity and abject humanity. We
have to find out what God's will is by standing up to
him and putting questions. This includes the possibilities
of being wrong and impious which have to be accepted
by anybody who is going to do anything seriously. We
must therefore insist on the validity of the intervening
time of seeking to know what devotion really is, and to
insist on it as being central to the whole business. The
same warning applies here as in dealing with the moment
of recognition. If this is to be genuine we must control
our instinct to be in too much of a hurry to get it right,
lest 'right' in that context mean forcing it into our values
and techniques.

The majestic dignity of the enlightened view is
enough to frighten us into accepting it. It is so much
purer than the sort of praying which usually goes on.
But it is not usually the best theology which captures its
audiences by scaring them. That is itself a good reason

for resisting it. Another is that the Christian tradition, in scripture and liturgy, contains a wealth of open and passionate asking, of people in particular adversity calling on God for particular help. When Phillips says that 'these prayers are far nearer superstition: kissing a rabbit's foot or touching wood' he may have made us angry enough to want to look at the whole thing again in hope of a more sympathetic understanding.

We can begin by opposing the enlightened puritans with the view of a weightier writer. Rudolf Bultman in *Jesus and the Word* insists that 'petition is the proper concern of a man who rightly understands his position before God. If he wished to give up prayers of petition because of the idea of omnipotence, then he would be arrogating to himself a knowledge of God which he does not possess.' We will move on by re-examining the idea of omnipotence in a Christian context and then look at some actual prayers.

The reservations of religious-philosophical writers about petition spring from an understandable chariness about mechanical notions of the powers of prayer. They are unwilling to believe in a God who intervenes in the world in a violent and arbitrary fashion, as if his own creation were not good enough for him. Even more distasteful is the idea that God is brought to act in this high-handed manner by the force of our praying, one magic act setting another in motion. Anybody will sympathise and agree with that. Where we differ is in seeing it as a signal, not to attack petitionary praying

but to question false and all-too-human notions of power.
'You know what impresses me most in this world?' asked
Napoleon in a moment of gloomy clarity. 'It is the
absolute inability of force to achieve anything.' He
should have known. We want a different understanding
of power, and Paul's first letter to the Corinthians
presents us with one.

It seems that in the Christian community at Corinth,
Paul was confronting a group which had got carried
away by its own intellectual and spiritual powers which
they demonstrated by speaking in tongues and isolating
themselves from the more ordinary Christian people. This
kind of superiority, with its appeal to being in the know
(they called it 'gnosis', wisdom), is religion at its worst
and most oppressive. The small stone from the brook
which Paul has ready to bring it to its knees and its
senses is the gospel of the cross. What has that central
Christian thing to do with intellectual or religious
majesty? It is the reverse and reversal of all that is
usually understood by power, folly to Greeks and dis-
graceful to Jews. Yet it is the power and the wisdom of
God. What is Paul talking about? Mystery certainly,
but understandable up to a point. In his own way he is
developing a strand of teaching which had already
become traditional and attached itself to the verse of the
old psalm 'the stone which the builders rejected has
become the headstone of the corner; this is the Lord's
doing and it is marvellous in our eyes'. To explain themselves at all the first Christians had to make some sense

of the brutal fact that the Messiah in whom they saw the focus of God's ways with men had died in a way which made him a worldly and religious failure. To hold on to this entailed nothing less than an overturning of worldly and religious values.

If we apply this to our thinking about power in prayer we may find a way out of the rational impasse. We think of power as the ability to move other people about from a distance while ourselves remaining inviolate. It sometimes works, but even in international politics its failures are more monumental. Its opposite accepts the very things which it rejects. It gives itself away without reserve, though certainly not in a resigned or passive way, and works by being with the other instead of over and above him. In the religious field its successes include the Samaritans and the contemplatives who work by an unconditional and interested being-with another.

According to Christian doctrine God and man belong together in a kind of power which looks like weakness and a kind of understanding that looks like foolishness since (unlike our usual view of understanding) it does not overwhelm, control or solve its object. It is something that can be experienced but not, by its very nature, analysed in a final way. It is the theme of Dylan Thomas's poem 'There was a Saviour' which is about the opening of feeling and communication in people who 'could not stir one lean sigh', whose compassion had become frozen in self-pity. It takes its cue from the kind of power that we have been looking at: 'Now in the

c

dark there is only yourself and myself' and reaches its
release and conclusion when

> Exiled in us we arouse the soft,
> Unclenched, armless, silk and rough love which
>   breaks all rocks.

Every word tells. 'Unclenched' and 'armless' are non-
power words, silk is in-between being soft but tough,
the roughness and the breaking of the rocks are symbols
of aggression and power. Like Paul, Thomas knows that
the two sides belong together. Asking is one of the points
at which they do so.

Asking is different from commanding and threatening
on the one hand and submission and resignation on the
other. It slips between the two sides of the argument
about petition. It is not the sort of rude and crude magic
which sensitive people find so offensive. Neither is it the
relieving of worried feelings or the instant resignation
to the will of another which they, in reaction, prefer.
It is something different and itself. When we ask somebody for something we are not merely declaring a state
of affairs, though that may be included. Still less are we
trying to improve our agitated minds by having it out,
though that too may be part of it. Those are not the
thing itself. They are not really asking. Nor, on the
other hand, are we trying to manoeuvre the other person
into doing exactly what we want by trapping him in
our powerful words and argument. If that happens, asking has lost its nature by changing into ordering. Having

become clear about what it is not, we must try to see what it is.

The question is: is praying to someone an attempt to change his mind and does it work? As with so many questions the answer depends on how and why it is being asked. The answer is 'no' if there is any trace of commanding in the asking. Genuine asking observes and respects the other's freedom of decision and keeps its distance. It is a discourse between two centres of freedom. In Homer's Iliad, for example, old King Priam pleads with Achilles for the dead body of his son Hector. He is in desperate earnest so he uses all the techniques of persuasion. He asks Achilles to think of his own father —an appeal to imaginative compassion. He clasps Achilles's knees, the seat of power. But he remains a king and a free man. He keeps his dignity by respecting Achilles's dignity. He recognises that he is in the presence of a free agent and does not resort to threatening or blackmail or hysteria. He is exercising what Nédoncelle calls a 'mutual influence that combines a mutual power to affect and also an individual freedom'. He draws short of some of the ways in which he might get what he wants because he is asking. But the answer to the question of whether he is trying to influence Achilles is 'yes' in the sense that he is presenting his case as powerfully as possible. He does everything he can to make clear the human and rational validity of his case. He holds back nothing in presenting himself and his need. He wants Achilles to understand it, attend to it and act upon it.

If we reduce what is going on here to a diagram it is that conjunction of two poles which is fundamental to our inquiry. There is a distance and a space between them which cannot be abolished without loss to them both. But it can be bridged by a community of interest, and it is precisely this which asking attempts to make. It is an appeal to the belonging-together of two distinct persons, an attempt to make that belonging-together real in a particular instance.

When somebody prays he expresses himself and his needs in a free and uninhibited way. The only restraint he acknowledges is that his prayer should allow an equally free and uninhibited answer. He seeks to move the other. He asks God to see and to act, but he leaves to him just how he should see and just how he should act. There is no grovelling. Like the early Christians he makes his plea standing upright on his feet. In this sense he is strong and active. But he does not attempt to control the answer, which rests with God. In this sense he is helpless. The difference is clear if we compare two prayers, one by Martin Luther and the other from a Zulu source.

Luther's prayer echoes the sentiments we often find in the psalms :

'Do good to me O Lord for thy name's sake. Thou knowest that the matter toucheth thee; thy name, thy word, thy honour. I praise but they blaspheme. If thou desertest me, thou forsakest thy name; but that is not possible, therefore deliver me!'

That is certainly uninhibited. Perhaps it is too bantering for refined tastes. But at the same time it observes a discipline. The control which Luther obeys is at the same time the ground for his pleading. It is God's name, by which he meant his free revealing of himself in the story of Israel and Jesus Christ. There he has chosen to commit himself to men to rescue and deliver them and establish them in freedom. He has bound himself to them in a community of interest. Luther is insisting on nothing more nor less than an endorsement of that. He is asking for an instance of the fact that God is not without man. He is holding a mirror up to God, his name, so as to move him to remember, see and act. Nothing that he says is an infringement on God's divinity, or his own lively humanity.

The Zulu prayer is like this up to a point, but without the control. As with Luther, the God is addressed in good, sound terms, but he is also threatened:

> 'When have we failed to sacrifice and repeat thy titles of honour? Why art thou then so niggardly? If thou dost not amend we will let all thy titles of honour fall into forgetfulness. What then will be thy fate? Then thou canst go and eat grasshoppers! Do better else we will forget thee! What is the good of our sacrificing and praising thee with all thy titles? Thou dost not render us any thanks for all our trouble.'

The way in which we petition God is determined by

what sort of a God we understand him to be. It is quite
clear that the Zulu God is so caught up in the destinies
of his worshippers that he is submerged in them. When it
comes to the crunch he does not have any independent
being, or if he has it is only of a very debilitated sort,
sustained by a diet of grasshoppers. His supplicants have
power over him and can threaten him with near-
extinction. He is vulnerable to blackmail, a dependent on
human magic. The Zulus have their sympathisers in
those modern churchmen who behave as if the destinies
of the kingdom of God depend on their own arrange-
ments. Their cult-idol should never be mistaken for the
God of Abraham, Isaac and Jacob, the father of Jesus
Christ.

The contrast between these two examples has marked
off genuine petitionary prayer from the magic sort. It
is the theology which makes the difference. One is very
plain and devoid of mystery. The god is the tribe, his
future the same as theirs. The other hangs on to a revelation which, largely because it happens in a story of a
free alliance, remains mysterious in the sense that it
cannot be overcome or pushed about. Yet Luther's prayer
is very different from the whittled down self-improve-
ment and submission to fate of the enlightened critics.
There can be no doubt that he is really asking God to
do something. Rudolf Bultmann, standing in that tradition, puts it clearly : 'modern interpretations of prayer
as an inner reconciliation with fate, a reverent submission
to the purposes of God, are far removed from Jesus; his

belief in prayer involves the union of trustful petition
with the will to surrender.'

There is one thing that Luther's prayer has in common
with the Zulu one and that is whole-heartedness, the
virtue behind all virtues which is threatened by the
implied moralism of the enlightened view. Sincerity is
the first requirement of petitionary prayer. In dealing
with contemplation we noticed that without it we have
lost before we start. We must not pretend to be other
than we are. This applies with particular force to the
vital area of our needs. They are the key to a personality.
A false or distorted view of them leads to the kind of
disorder which can result in a nervous breakdown. Again,
a determined act of resistance is needed. When high-
minded men start telling us what we ought to want we
should summon up the courage to take G. K. Chesterton's
sound advice :

> If an angel out of heaven
> Brings you other things to drink,
> Thank him for his kind attentions,
> Go and pour them down the sink.

or John Burnaby's more temperate doctrine in
Soundings : 'if I am to learn what God wants, the way to
do it is not to disown the inmost desires of my heart, but
rather deliberately to spread them out before God—to
face with all the honesty I can achieve the real truth
about my desires, to wrestle with the sham of professing

desires which are not really mine.' Traditional material comes to our aid. If there is one thing that is certain about the message of Jesus it is that it met people at their point of need. It is precisely there that the mysterious good news of the kingdom of God takes effect and becomes real—to the great distress of the possessors and custodians of theological and moral certainty. His work and message was baffled only when it met those who had no genuine needs or refused to acknowledge them. The right man is the disreputable publican who pleads for mercy rather than the pharisee who counts his blessings like a miser fingering his gold—'mine, all mine!' as Winnie-the-Pooh said in one of his sillier moments. Such people are included by the gospel, not under the blessing given to the poor but the curse pronounced over the rich. This central Christian doctrine encourages even Luther's importunity.

Need and asking are so essential to being human that any watering down of it, let alone denial, is crippling. If we chose to take as normative the person who does not seriously want things and ask for them we should not be dealing with humanity. Nobody has known that better than the obscure West Country clergyman Thomas Traherne. He made it the foundation of the theology of his *Centuries*. Unfortunately he expressed himself with such luminous felicity (sometimes in verse) that his works are put on the 'English Literature' shelves of the libraries where theologians seldom go except off duty. He sees human need as the door to human happiness. Take it seriously, refuse to be fobbed off with the substitutes with which stupid people try to satisfy it, and you are on the way to heaven. His text might be the verse from the psalm 'open thy mouth wide, and I will fill it'. 'Wants,' he says, 'are the ligatures which tie us to God, whereby we live in him and feel his enjoyments.' That is his doctrine of man, whose fulfilment consists in wanting and having his needs met. Those who never want anything are never happy.

It is in his doctrine of God that Traherne makes a move daring enough to take our breath away and make us fear for his orthodoxy. In dealing with understanding in the first chapter we noticed that knowledge is most itself when it is mutual—'then shall I know even as I am known'. Traherne thinks the same about wanting. Most notions about God are offensively boring because they depict him as a complacent being who has got every-thing. There is nothing that he seriously wants. Though dull and dignified enough to excite unenthusiastic respect, such a God is dismissed by Traherne as heathen and dead, 'but the Lord God of Israel, the living and true God, was from all Eternity, and from all Eternity wanted like a God'. What did he want? People to enjoy his divin-ity, worlds, spectators, joys and treasures. Somewhat taken aback by his own thinking Traherne says 'This is very strange that God should want, for in him is the fullness of blessedness'. But he finds that no objection. God is always wanting and always satisfied. How else could he be happy? The two belong together. 'He is from all

D

eternity full of want, or else he could not be full of treasure.' 'Want is the fountain of all his fullness.'

Traherne has never had his due from the theologians. This is a pity because his lively teaching does justice to the central Christian conviction that God is love and that he who abides in love abides in God. All too often the orthodox thinkers have been embarrassed by this at the same time as they rhapsodise over its excellence. Perhaps it is the age-old Christian distrust of sex that has led them to try to dissociate the love of God from any trace of passionate desire. The result is unappetising and incredible since love without that is something that we cannot imagine and may well not want to. Was Stanley Spencer nearer the truth when he found it 'difficult to imagine a sexless heaven' and depicted God in the likeness of his father, encouraging the lovers in the bedroom? The image is not as outrageous as it appears. Writers in the Old and New Testaments perhaps went further in feeling free to picture God and Christ as husband and bridegroom. Presumably they meant what they said. *Honi soit qui mal y pense.* Desire and wanting are as serious and indispensable a part of loving as the equally important aspects which theologians usually prefer, tender care and disinterested delight. The same applies to prayer, which Paul described as an inward groaning, longing for the redemption of our bodies. But the bowdlerisers have been at work on petition too.

If we dare to take Traherne's insight seriously we are on the threshold of an illuminating discovery. There are passages in the Old Testament which quite explicitly describe God's relation to people as being one of petition and prayer. He yearns for Israel and stretches out his hands to her in the attitude of the supplicant. 'All the day long have I stretched out my hands to a disobedient and gainsaying people.' He draws or attracts them with cords of compassion and bands of love. He prays to them. If it is right to think of God's being and activity as subject to any law, it is the law of love which desires its object yet exerts no other power over it than the power of a constant and pleading presence which never destroys its freedom. In more customary language, he calls us. Asking is the way in which God and man belong together. God gives man freedom and recognises it by asking things of him rather than forcing them out of him. Man acknowledges God's freedom in the same way. If neither ever asked he would not be really interested.

The teaching of the New Testament does not do away with this but confirms it. Its first and last conviction is that God came to men in Jesus Christ. The supplicant, like the widow in the parable presents himself and his case. With daring self-committal he allows his honour and even his future to rest in the hands of others, as lovers do. He adventures himself with us. So God in Christ is given up into the hands of wicked men so that he can declare himself and they can do as they will with him. In Christian doctrine Jesus Christ is God's prayer to the world, which is the same as saying that he is God's love to the world.

In the first chapter we used the analogies of becoming interested in a picture or a person and found that there was something there before the awakening of our interest. There was a beginning before our beginning. Here is something after the same pattern. Before our beseeching of God is God's beseeching of us. He, as the author of the covenant alliance, sets the terms which are appropriate to it and to the behaviour of both its parties. It must work itself out in the discourse between two centres of freedom which is genuine petitionary prayer. Discourse is a weak word for an exchange in which so much is at stake. It is, in fact, only safe for a man to put his life in the hands of another if that other will in his turn do the same towards him. How can he be sure that he will? Only by faith and by testing. These are the subject of the next chapter.

CHAPTER FOUR

The Dark Wood

'I say, Jeeves, I met a man at the club last night
who told me to put my shirt on Privateer for the
two o'clock race this afternoon. How about it?'
'I would not advocate it, sir. The stable is not
sanguine.'
'Talking about shirts, Jeeves, have those mauve ones
I ordered come yet?'
'Yes, sir. I sent them back.'
'Sent them back?'
'Yes, sir. They would not have become you.'

P. G. Wodehouse

For the Lord had said to Moses, 'Say to the people
of Israel: "You are a stiff-necked people; if for a
single moment I should go up among you, I would
consume you. So now put off your ornaments from
you, that I may know what to do with you." '

Exodus 33, 5

And all shall be well
All manner of thing shall be well
By the purification of the motive
In the ground of our beseeching.

T. S. Eliot

THE LAST CHAPTER CRITICISED THOSE THEORIES ABOUT
praying which play down the role of asking in the

interests of submission to the will of God. Trying to be
right too quickly can be the same thing as being wrong.
The trouble with those devout and rational opinions
was that they refused to take seriously the inquiry and
testing which must precede a proper and creative act
of submission, which without them could have some of
the character of an act of high-minded impatience with
divinity and humanity. It stops the game before it has
really started. It says little for the determination or
freedom of the participants if they allow that to happen,
and the final result is correspondingly featureless. We
need to remind ourselves of the basic things of theology.
It is interested in God and man, vision and sober reality.
It believes that the two belong together. But it also
insists on the distance and difference between them.
That is its fascination and its difficulty. Short cuts and
instant solutions have to be avoided because they do not
work. In the end they lead to boredom and confusion
—an unappetising combination. We are still in the
kitchen and, for the sake of the quality of the dish and
the proper nourishment of the family, we must refuse
to be hustled.

*   *   *

The belonging-together of God and man makes itself
felt in two convictions which are with us all the time.
The first is that I am never alone. Try as I may to
isolate myself and be a private citizen, other people and
other things are always interrupting me and calling for

my attention. The second is that I am alone too much. There is an irreducible loneliness and separation which resists all my attempts to dissolve it and obsesses me with the problem of communication. My individuality springs from others and is fed by relation with them, yet they remain others and I remain myself. As the businessman complained to his wife, even my secretary does not understand me.

Logically these two convictions exclude one another. They cannot both be true. But in experience they can often come together. Standing on the hill top, looking at somebody or listening to music can catch us in a mixture of satisfaction and longing for which bitter-sweet is too pretty an adjective. It touches the fundamental religious discovery that man is at home in two worlds yet believes that the world is one—or could be. These simultaneous feelings amount to a sense that this is mine and me, and yet not mine and entirely itself. Because of this I think of myself as someone who is looking for the place where he belongs and the goodness of being recognised by another. For this reason contemplation, as described in the first chapter, does not settle me into the armchair. It emerges as an invitation to explore further into the world and God. That is what all my loving, working and praying are about. If I give up the search I deny myself without following Jesus. If I mislead or obstruct other people in their search I injure them badly.

The thing that is being sought is very simple. It is promised in Gabriel Oak's proposal to Bathsheba in

Far from the Madding Crowd: 'whenever you look up, there shall I be—and whenever I look up, there will be you.' In the Christian story the life of Jesus rests on this mutual recognition and consists in working it out. He says 'Father' and God replies 'You are my son'. But for all its simplicity it is hard to get it right, as the history of doctrine in the first centuries of Christianity shows.

Debate about the nature of Christ in the early church was long, passionate and complicated. One sometimes wonders what it was all about, why they went to such trouble and got so heated and aggressive. The answer is that in discussing Christ they were trying to find a way of putting how God and man belong together. Christ-ology is the focus in which a Christian does his theology. Nothing matters more than getting it right. It was a job done under the pressure of formulations of the doctrine of Christ which looked plausible and logical yet threatened to tip the whole thing off the rails. In a world seething with religious and philosophical specula-tion there was bound to be a bewildering variety of interpretations, each of them proclaimed with passionate intensity because it expressed the way in which its adherents saw their world—natural and supernatural. It was the articulation of their deepest hopes, fears and convictions. A bitter disgust with the world is compen-sated by an insistence on the purer realm of the kingdom of God and emerges in an emphasis on Christ's divinity rather than his humanity. A greater optimism about man and nature would take the argument the other way.

Often the trouble was not so much with what people said as with what they failed, or refused, to say. Insistence on one aspect or the other was an assertion of something essential to theology and prayer, but if it did so at the expense of its opposite it gave a false account which would result in banal spirituality and constricted ethics. A third option was to resolve the tricky tension by mixing the two poles of the argument together and making a divine man who was both rather more than human and rather less than God. In symbolic geography such a being is stuck in the religious mid-air between heaven and earth. More seriously, he stopped the game; and if one thing is certain it is that the game goes on.

To put it another way: the struggle was between dualism and monism. Dualism insists on the separation of the two worlds of divinity and humanity. If it is complete there can be no dialogue between the two. We have to escape from nature into God. There is no common language for communication. Monism does the other thing. It brings God and man so close together that you cannot get a knife between them. This is, quite literally, confusion. It too abolishes dialogue by making the two parties into one. If there is any talking it cannot be dialogue. It will be one person talking to himself. Christianity found itself by refusing to fall into either of these. It knew that God is God and man is man and ever more shall be so. At the same time it knew that they belonged together and that there was dialogue between these two centres of freedom. It is the same in a relation

D*

of two people. Romanticism might lead them to suppose
that they could become one person, entirely submerged
in one another. High-minded cynicism would tell them
that two people cannot live together and it is better not
to try. If they have any sense they will not fall for either
of those deceptive simplicities, either the rosy one or the
jaundiced one, but prefer the difficulties and promise
of the way of union without confusion.

The good theologian only speaks when silence would
be worse. The definition of Christ made at the Council
of Chalcedon in 451 was a refusal to be misled, a proclamation of the belonging-together of humanity and
divinity without either fudging or divorce. The language
is tortuous: 'of one substance with the Father as regards
his divinity, and at the same time of one substance with
us as regards his humanity. . . . One and the same
Christ . . . recognised in two natures without confusion,
without change, without separation: the distinction of
the two natures being in no way annulled by the union,
but rather the characteristics of each nature being pre-
served and coming together to form one person and
existence.' The Christian has a foot in two worlds yet
believes that the world is somehow one. The best way to
read that ancient dogma is in the light of Auden's maxim
that theological statements are like shaggy dog stories.
They have a point, but if you try too hard to get it you
will miss it.

The work done at Chalcedon allows God to be himself and to be in touch with his opposite. It does the

same for man. The trouble with it is that it is a formula and not a story. It is a static diagram of something which is always on the move. It points to a life which is unexpurgatedly human and unexpurgatedly divine, preferring the things of God and the things of man to religious tidiness. That is an invigorating prospect. Yet it is only a still outside the cinema. For the real thing we must buy a ticket and go inside. What will that be?

Comedy, like theology, is made to a very simple recipe: the conjunction of opposites. It is made by putting together two situations or people which are usually thought to be apart. Jokes are its simplest examples. The dignified fat man puts his foot on the banana skin. Finding his wife in bed with a cardinal, the Count walks deliberately across the room, throws up the window and blesses the people in the street below: 'You, Monsignor, have assumed my duties, so I am performing yours.' Laughter is the fall-out of the explosion when two distinct things are pushed together. Comedy spins it out. Two people are brought together although they are different from one another in age, character or sex. They become a couple in spite of the contrast. The addition of other couples, similarly or differently contrasted, can add depth and intricacy to the drama but does not alter the basic structure. The most usual and obvious difference-cum-unity is sexual. *Vive la différence!* So a great many comedies are about a man and a woman in love, the battle of the sexes. Mozart and Giovanni da Ponte, his librettist, have given us glorious examples of it in *The Marriage of Figaro* and *Cosi Fan Tutte*. Patronising listeners who used to think of them as elegant froth have been proved wrong. To miss their deep seriousness about the human predicament is to miss the joke too. Shakespeare's *Much Ado about Nothing* and *A Winter's Tale* are on the same level. In *The Tempest* and *A Midsummer Night's Dream* there is the added dimension of a meeting of two contrasting realms and their effect on one another. With Falstaff and Prince Hal, character and age are the points of difference and relationship. This is given a twist by the clear fact that, for all his seniority Falstaff is really a baby, a little stranger in the world, whereas young Hal is already something of a Machiavellian prince and a wordly-wise politician. P. G. Wodehouse invented another immortal couple, Wooster and Jeeves. The provident and omniscient gentleman's gentleman appears as a God who has humbled himself and taken upon himself the form of a servant. His master's accident-prone improvidence and constant need of redemption by Jeeves can only remind us of ourselves. In any case, this was a recipe so pregnant with possibilities that it has carried through a great number of books. It has reminded us of the best conjunction of opposites of all, God and man—the theme of the Bible and Christian tradition. There could hardly be a stronger contrast or a more inseparable couple than that. Its comic character comes out unashamedly in the book of Jonah. In this biting satire on religious man Jonah's self-importance, self-preserva-

tion and resentful intransigence are put against God's
steadfast mercy and adaptability. As in all the others,
the story moves between two poles.

In all these examples it is essential that the two participants are bound together. Men and women are
mysterious to one another, psycho-sexual opposites, but
they need one another and cannot forget it. Old Falstaff
needs Hal's youth and Hal's jokes depend on his ungainly
age. The relationship dies when Hal becomes king, so
Falstaff dies too. He could not survive it. When he is
resurrected in *The Merry Wives of Windsor* he is a
shadow of his former self. Jeeves's discreet and efficient
realism and Wooster's feckless capacity for fantasy
enhance one another. We cannot imagine that Wooster
would prefer another valet or that Jeeves would like a
more sober master. In all these cases we cannot think of
one without the other. If we do, we bring about a sharp
decline in the comic temperature such as actually
occurred when Tony Hancock and Sid James dissolved
their partnership.

We do not have to alter the picture when we move
on to the Biblical couple. God is not without man. The
doctrines of creation, covenant and redemption present
a divinity who has chosen never to be without his opposite. He has always been *en rapport* with his creation,
and with man in particular. The alliance is indissoluble
and can never be broken. In dealing with petitionary
prayer we balanced the usual insistence on man's depen-
dence upon God with the doctrine of God's depend-

ence upon us. Certainly this is, in good traditional theology, voluntary. He has chosen that it should be so. It is none the less irrevocable. In the great comedy of Job it is God's own honour that is at stake in Satan's onslaught on Job's integrity and devotion. God stands to lose because he has adventured his glory and allowed it to stand or fall by a man. We could read the story of Jesus in a similar way, the Son of Man (which means God's agent) who is given into the hands of wicked men. It is because God is love that he becomes a participant in the comic ordeal. There would be no Christianity at all if he did not give himself over to us and pray to us, nor if we failed to do the same in return.

So far we have only anatomised the structure of comedy in a static diagram. But it contains the seeds of action and drama. Like Christian doctrine, comedy is not a theory but a story. It opens by presenting us with the characters and establishing how they belong together —or want to belong together. Then it goes on to tell the tale of how that relationship is worked out. In Genesis we are shown man created by God in his own image, that is, with a likeness to him and a community of interest with him. Then we are shown man trying to get away from his creator. 'The man and the woman hid themselves from the presence of the Lord God among the trees of the garden.' Gods calls to them 'Where are you?' It is a question. The business of asking which is central to Christianity and comedy has begun. More than that, it is a question which sums up the centre of the action, which is a seeking-out of the other through all kinds of evasion and disguise, up blind alleys and in the haunted forest. All this has to be gone through before the happy union which ends every comedy. Yet the relationship continues. It is not broken. In Genesis God continues to care for man and man continues to be responsible to God. Only the scene has changed. It is no longer the idyll of the happy encounter at the beginning. In the dark wood identities get shuffled and confused. The characters are driven near to madness, since being no longer clear about whom they are after entails being confused about their own identities. They are calling to one another 'Where are you?'.

What sense is there in this gruelling situation which lovers share with theologians and researchers?

In order to arrive at what you do not know
You must go by a way which is the way of ignorance.

A scientist notices something which does not fit the current theories. He decides to take it seriously. This is a brave step because it means that for a while he is going to be lost. He moves out of the familiar realm of certainty into an area of inquiry where nobody has been before. He will need all he can get of that fundamental virtue which is required of patients in hospital, lovers, parents and saints—the tolerance of uncertainty. He sails with the Jumblies. Like them, he undertakes all this for the sake of the discovery of reality. He could emerge having learned things which could not be learned in any other way. In Vanbrugh's comedy *The Relapse* Lord Foppington, an exquisite man of fashion, finds himself being rushed about a West Country farmyard in a wheelbarrow protesting 'This is a most impertinent dream!' He is thoroughly lost and confused, but the experience teaches him humility and humanity. He becomes more himself in the undignified process. We have several times noticed the necessity of sincerity in prayer. How does one achieve it? The answer must be that it is something learned in the inquisition of the comic ordeal. There the lover's vows of eternal devotion are tested against the fact that men and women are fickle creatures. In *Cosi Fan Tutte* Guglielmo and Ferrando, the impetuous wooers, take on a bet with Don Alfonso the ageing realist, that their women will be faithful to them. A plot is then devised, entailing the wearing of disguises, which will put this to an empirical test. The lovers swear by heaven. Don Alfonso swears by the earth. In the end it is acknowledged that everybody has failed—that's what they all do. Love remains, as St Paul said it would, but it is love on a more modest and human scale than the romantic rapture of the beginning because it has been through the fire. Heaven and earth are finally reconciled when everybody has made a fool of himself and forgiveness is all that is left —a happy ending.

The Christian at prayer cannot pretend that he still lives in the innocence of Eden or that he has yet reached the New Jerusalem. The discourse between him and

God is not yet resolved nor yet without mutual seeking. He too is in the dark wood, knowing all too well how Lysander feels in *A Midsummer Night's Dream* :

And here am I and wood (mad) within this wood
Because I cannot get my Hermia.

The irony there is that his destiny is not Hermia at all but Helena, his first love, whom he is trying to escape from and lose. There is a parallel here with Jonah, or with Israel in the prophecy of Hosea when God says :

Therefore I will hedge up her way with thorns
and I will build up a wall against her
so that she cannot find her paths.
She shall pursue her lovers,
but not overtake them,
and she shall seek them,
but not find them.
Then she shall say 'I will go
and return to my first husband,
for it was better with me then than now.'

The prodigal son came to the same conclusion by being put through the same trying circumstances. Life with God, the concern of theology and prayer, is a similar comedy, a game of hide and seek which is enacted on the brink of the precipice of tragedy with masks and disguises concealing the participants from one another.

But the agonising drama is framed and upheld by its

beginning and its end, the eternal alliance between God and man, heaven and earth. Neither party can forget or, in the end, evade the other. Job knew that life would be more restful if he could. We suffer from this inability to forget and so, according to Hosea, does God :

How can I give you up, O Ephraim?
    how can I hand you over, O Israel?
My heart recoils within me,
    my compassion grows warm and tender.

This restlessness is the mainspring of prayer, understood as a continual quest for our opposite, God, and his continual quest for us. We cannot give up and we will not be given up. It could be said that prayer means precisely holding in oneself the tension between heaven and earth, things as they are and things as they could be. Anyone who prays is taking seriously Stanley Spencer's vivid creed 'I am on the side of angels and dirt', or E. M. Forster's more sober injunction 'Only connect the poetry and the prose and both will be exalted'. He also takes the consequences of that conviction.

Throughout this investigation we have insisted on the fundamental simplicity which underlies it all. Divinity and humanity have been its subject, a God who is never without man and a man who is never without God. The earliest Christians lived on that and their faithfulness to it entailed a happy disregard of much that was thought to be true religion. Their irreverence for ethical and pious clutter brought them under suspicion of being impious and libertine. Life had been stripped down to its bare essentials, God and man and their belonging-together, and so ste free. Their achievement was to affirm the validity of the creature in his earthiness and of the creator in his divinity. They believed in angels and dirt, an alliance between God as he is and people as they are which left no place for demi-gods and religion. The focus of it all was the cross which stands in the middle of the dark wood. For them, that was the place of the alliance. That serves to remind us of the second conviction that we have held to in this inquiry, that the simplicity is not cheap and does not excuse us from getting lost and being wrong. It is a 'condition of complete simplicity, costing not less than everything'. Its attraction should never lead us to imagine that we can get to it by short cuts which avoid the trials of the story which it belongs to. Simplicity is not the devout man's fancy-dress. Marie Antoinette did not become a peasant by putting on a straw hat and playing with a hay rake. The real issues were elsewhere, demanding more serious and expensive treatment. It is a pity to learn that too late.

The comic ordeal is the setting of everything that we have examined. It is an old and traditional story which is told again and again in a variety of literary and living forms. Its content is petitionary prayer, the only way in which two distinct and different centres of freedom can work out their community of interest. Its discipline and aim is the cleansing of the doors of perception until we know even as we are known. It is a grim and gruelling business, but none the less a comedy for that. In consequence the Christian life, which consists of a lively and inquiring love of God and a lively and inquiring love of the world and people, should be marked by an incurable seriousness and an incurable lightness—what Barth has called 'a certain earnestness and humour'. Theology is the gayest and most serious of studies. Its practitioners (who are by no means confined to the writers and readers of religious books) should always irritate and delight by their good-humoured mockery of much that religious and wordly men take seriously, their earnestness about much that they neglect or ridicule. The disciple should be like salt in the world because the God who pursues him and whom he pursues is the joker in the pack.

The Christian Thing

'He is the image of the invisible God, the first born of all creation; for in him all things were created, in heaven and on earth, visible and invisible, whether thrones or dominions or principalities or authorities—all things were created in him and for him. He is before all things, and in him all things hold together. He is the head of the body, the church; he is the beginning, the first-born from the dead, that in everything he might be pre-eminent. For in him all the fullness of God was pleased to dwell, and through him to reconcile all things to himself, whether on earth or in heaven, making peace by blood of his cross.'

Colossians 1, 15-20

'I want to try and speak for a class of Christian believers who have the utmost difficulty in summoning up much interest in the historical Jesus. . . . For some of us Christ has no meaning until we see him in our contemporaries. We are like deaf people who have missed some very important communication and then are shown it written down. I can only believe in repentance or forgiveness or love or resurrection when others near to me show it to me, which, believer or nonbeliever, they unfailingly do. But then the gospels become something infinitely precious, a faithful distilling of the essence of being human which is beyond all price.'

Monica Furlong

THE PHILOSOPHER BERNARD WILLIAMS HAS PUT THE TASK
of theology in a sentence. It must 'show how religious
language can gear into other language, and must lay
bare the points of intersection'. That is precisely what
we have been trying to do in this investigation. But
Williams took a gloomy view of the outcome of this
exercise: 'in the end it cannot be successful in this;
for the points of intersection . . . must contain something incomprehensible.' Again we agree. The whole
business has been an attempt to discover markers
which point to a central mystery. But has it been successful? That depends on what kind of success is expected,
which in turn depends on the nature of the material we
have used. When a sculptor works on a piece of wood or
stone he simultaneously changes it into something else
and lets it be itself. He overcomes it and respects it. If his
efforts are successful he will leave behind something
which, by the marriage of his own lively vision to the life
and nature of the material, has a mysterious life of its
own. A painter loves his paint and wants it to look like
paint as well as the object it represents. Success consists in
an alliance of overcoming and letting be, which gives
birth to something new, indefinable and real.

The material of theology is the mystery of the intersection of two worlds, so it too 'must contain something
incomprehensible'. It therefore expresses itself in hints,
points and even jokes. It never actually gets us there.
It does not deliver the goods, but it suggests where the
goods are to be found. The media it uses suit its message

by indicating something which cannot be contained or finally put in its place. It never reaches the kind of comprehension which amounts to mastery over its subject by the abolition of its mysterious material—the final solution. 'How small a whisper do we hear of him. We touch but the outskirts of his ways.' It accepts and exploits the fact that there is 'something incomprehensible' at the centre of its discipline, just as there is in any long-standing and intimate relationship between two people. There too, the refusal to acknowledge and tolerate the fact is a recipe for disaster. In Bartók's opera *Bluebeard's Castle* the young bride's refusal to acknowledge the distance between herself and her strange husband, her insistence on unlocking all the doors and knowing everything, ends inevitably in loneliness and death. Yet there is a kind of understanding which is liberating and not destructive. The neglect of that, through cynicism or timidity, is equally tragic.

The two poles of theological inquiry are God and man. Both of them will always be subjects of inquiry because we do not fully understand them. They keep their secrets and their freedom. Yet we work from the presupposition that both of them, because love is in their natures, have given themselves away to the other in some measure—and indeed as completely as their being allows. The incomprehensibility is qualified although it is not abolished.

Man was the starting point because most of us know more about the mystery of humanity than of divinity.

As a matter of historical fact and record there have always been people looking for the kingdom of God in its points of intersection with the more familiar world, and they have usually been moved to it because the more familiar world strikes them as odder than is generally believed. They have wanted to establish themselves in that other world which Muir called the fable and to leave signs of their presence there in writings, images or social work. These are not just the people who are usually listed as theologians, and if all that they have left behind them are sign-posts pointing towards some mysterious centre, footprints petering out towards the desert or wreckage washed up on the beach, these are still worth looking at. They are indicators of something which has a primacy over and above all their efforts and of a beginning before their beginnings, witnesses to one who is mightier than they and who prevails.

So it is that when they speak they tell of something which, unlike themselves, has always been there : 'the life was made manifest and we saw it and testify to it'. They insist that it was not really they who began the business but the other. Their part was to thread their way back through the labyrinth to the source or *datum* of the one who was there all the time, revealing himself and making himself clear in a thousand ways which all added up to something unified and real which they cannot pin down. They experienced a home-coming. If there is undoubtedly no place like home, it is also true that it is an impossible place to describe to those who have not been

there, and even to those who have. The name has to
suffice by its power to recall memories and obscure
meanings. As with theology, descriptions of it are best
left like that or put as invitations to come and stay. In
either case something interrogatory, a question mark,
hangs obstinately to the statement.

The incomprehensibility of talk about God is relieved
if we attend sympathetically to those who say that they
have known something of him. To do that we must not
mistake their tone of voice or their intentions. They
speak a language which holds the mystery while letting
it be itself, like a setting to a precious stone. To achieve
this they have to practise the sort of precision which is
demanded of poets, struggling to arrange words around
a silence, images around an invisibility, in a way which
will uphold the central thing strongly and clearly but
never confound it by changing its nature into something
without mystery. That is what the theologians at Chalcedon were trying to do.

Christians have always regarded Jesus as the central,
definitive and even final revelation of the God who is
not without man. In his words and deeds, and above all
in his death and resurrection, the kingdom of God has
been revealed once for all. Are they right? It may seem
irritating to insist that it all depends on how they say it
and on their tone of voice and yet, as in private conver-
sations, it is precisely that which can make all the difference between something life-giving and something death-
dealing. The same remark can be an insult or an

encouragement. To treat God's revelation of himself in Christ as something final and plain in an aggressively authoritarian way, to use it as a club for dealing out apostolic blows and knocks, can never be an expression of faith. More usually it reveals the kind of unresolved muddle which expresses itself in a bogus simplicity. On the question of divorce, for instance, some Christian theologians may wish to invoke the words of Jesus on the subject in order to settle the matter and put an end to taxing argument. They run into the initial difficulty that the gospels do not agree about what he said and that no amount of wrenching and twisting will get them to agree. Probably they ignore the fact that society has changed between now and then so that the things which uphold or threaten it could have altered too. That would compound the difficulty. But it could be that the refusal of this most important question to yield to a final solution is the key to the whole thing. Following Biblical tradition we have seen in the relations of man and woman an image of the belonging-together of God and man: a constant mutual exploration upheld by a mysterious, even arbitrary, mutual commitment and faithfulness which allows the other his freedom. It combines attachment and letting-go, taking for granted and taking nothing for granted. No regulations, conservative or permissive, can have the final word on something which leads people into the faithfulness, freedom and forgiveness of God: that, made real in a particular situation, can be the only arbiter. Nothing less will do it without damage to humanity and divinity; and it imposes its own searching discipline.

The conviction that God has revealed himself in Jesus will, if it is genuine and creative, be a gateway to exploration rather than a command that it should stop. Only so can it share in the character of primitive Christianity, which was a renaissance of ethics, imagination, thinking, story-telling and worship—all the elements which make up theology revived by a new wonder and simplicity. The point of intersection was a point of departure.

When God reveals himself he still remains himself; that is, he still transcends our analysis and definition. Revelation opens a hole in the dividing wall through which he can be seen and addressed. It is not a cage in which he is caught, thereafter to be the pet of religious people. It makes him immediate, it even makes him ours, but it does not finish him off. He still has to be sought. Like God, Jesus escapes our impatient lust for objective certainty. Like father, like son.

The New Testament contains four versions of his life. They often agree. In the first instance this is because they depend on the same historical story: that he proclaimed the immediacy of God in word and action, that he was crucified, but that his death was not the end but the beginning. In the second instance the accounts agree because none of them (not even John's) was written in complete independence of the others. Copying accounts for many of the agreements. One gospel

could be a source of another. But then we are struck by
the disagreements. His last words and circumstances of
his birth are matters of obvious interest and importance,
yet there are three different versions of the former and
two of the latter. Matthew's Christmas stories are quite
different from Luke's with only a few agreements. In
Mark and Matthew, Jesus dies with a cry of desperate
loss, in Luke with serene words of commital, in John
with a triumphant 'It is finished'. More than that, each
Gospel has its own distinctive character, resulting in a
distinctive Christ who is not identical with the Christ of
the other writers. William Blake saw the point long ago:

> The vision of Christ which thou dost see
> Is my vision's greatest enemy.
> Thine has a great hook nose like thine;
> Mine has a snub nose like mine.
> Thine is the friend of all mankind;
> Mine speaks in parables to the blind.

Mark's Christ speaks in parables to the blind. Even his
disciples can no more understand him than they can
forget him. In Luke's book he is the friend of all man-
kind, making his message clear in sublime common-sense
and plain tales. In Matthew's version he is a new kind
of divine rabbi, much concerned with the contrasts and
likenesses between his own theology and ethics and those
of traditional law-abiding Judaism. In John's he is the
self-expression of God, eternal judge and life-giver,
speaking the exalted language of mystical illumination.

The individuality of the gospels defies homogenisation.

The contrasts between them have been put boldly because so many interpreters have tried to reduce them to one standard product, a sort of theological *Liebfraumilch* or *vin ordinaire* in which Luke's more human and plausible portrait is usually the main ingredient. But suppose we follow our rule of rejoicing in the individuality and peculiarity of the material and work with it rather than against it? Suppose we again take as our text the psalmist's praise of diversity: 'Lord, how manifold are thy works: in wisdom hast thou made them all!' This will entail a refusal to hustle and hector the witnesses, a willingness to let them say what they want to say rather than what we want them to say. We follow Wittgenstein's advice to look before we think, with the added conviction that divine inspiration does not abolish a man's inventiveness or his individuality (not even an evangelist's) but enhances it. We have to tolerate a suspense before the great question of who Jesus was, but we do so in order to come to a fresh and more appropriate understanding. This is a vast, if delightful, programme of work. What sort of an understanding and a certainty may we hope to reach if we follow it? The answer must be provisional and (again) individual, but here it is.

It was said earlier that Christology, the discussion about who Jesus is, is the focus in which Christians do their theology. Through that lens they scrutinise the belonging-together of divinity and humanity in its past, present and future aspects, the ways of God with men and of men with God. The question is: why this particular lens, why him? The answer which best explains the new life which began with him is that his life expressed this belonging-together with a sharp immediacy which could only be greeted as quite right or quite wrong, as either perfect or shocking. Looking at him or listening to him was to be brought uncomfortably close to God—or was it the devil? To those entrenched in the status quo and holding large investments in it the latter seemed more likely: he was a demonic threat to everything by which they ordered their lives and made sense of themselves. He presented an uncertainty and a mystery which they could not stand. To those who, for one reason or another, were still open and searching, he presented the only hope and certainty. In either case, he brought people to the edge where this world touches another. He gave them real theology.

Primitive Christianity was a rediscovery of God; according to its own conviction, a rediscovery or redemption of the world by God, who is the beginning before our beginning. In going back to the eternal alliance which is at the root of religion it had little reverence or interest for the paraphernalia. When the central thing re-asserts itself and the springs of the waters are seen, peripheral matters are put in their place. They are secondary, in spite of those who insist that they are primary because they do not trust the centre. Christianity came as a great passing-away of the Gods. The religious Valhalla went up in flames, the ornate and stuffy scenery melted away and there was nothing on

the stage except a man (a degraded and rejected man
at that) and the voice of God saying 'This is my son'.
Around this mysterious simplicity, discovered through so
much pain, misunderstanding and storm, life began
anew. Theology, by being done in terms of it, became
Christology. It was in Jesus that they knew the God
who is not without man.

The New Testament was written in the heat and
excitement of that new discovery. It need not surprise
us that it has the enthusiasm and individuality of a
collection of love-letters by different hands. It is the fall
out of laughter, expressing wonder and delight at the
sudden conjunction of two opposites. In consequence it
is full of the heart-felt exaggeration which comes from
people who have been overtaken by a radical happiness
—this is the thing, this is what life is about, look!

It follows that we are strangers to the original
Christianity if we read its documents as the dry, normative definitions of an orthodoxy, an excuse to stop
searching for the kingdom. If we do we shall, ironically,
have put ourselves in precisely the same position as those
people who could not take Jesus and his message in the
first place because it did not slot easily into received
religious opinion. We shall have missed the all-important
tone of voice of the first Christians and so misunderstood
them by reading them at the wrong temperature. A
sinister change has occurred when 'This is it!' is no
longer said in wonder, worship and avid curiosity but as
an expression of complacent authority which fears new-

ness and discovery : 'Go and find out what the children are doing and tell them to stop it.' Theology is then no longer a risky exploration where everything is at stake. It is an intellectual game which is perfectly safe so long as you play it by the accepted rules. In the realm of work another ominous change will have taken place : the theologian's task will have been cut away from the saint's, and on the library shelves spirituality will have become a different class from doctrine. Worst of all, head and heart will have become alienated from one another : the neurotic recipe for short-term comfort and long-term disaster which Freud unmasked.

This book has attempted to go the other way. In try- ing to explore a few of the points of intersection at which the divine and the human belong together it has moved, in the company of poets and others, in the realms of present experience. In consequence it has been attached only loosely to abstract philosophy and even more loosely to the desire to make everything specifically and pecu- liarly Christian. If Christian faith is true, then its adherents can relax in order to work all the better. They can rove about in the confidence that they will find its truth in a number of unlikely and forbidden places. They can look forward to the shattering surprise which Paul experienced when the two opposites clicked together in his mind and he saw the righteousness and power of God in a condemned and helpless man. And set off on his travels and lived happily, if strenuously, ever after.